A Taste of Life
by Rexella Van Impe

All Scripture quotations are from the King James Version of the Bible.

Copyright © 1995 by Jack Van Impe Ministries.

All rights reserved. Written permission must be secured from publisher to use or reproduce any part of this book, except for brief quotations in critical reviews or articles.

Printed in the United States of America.

Jack Van Impe Ministries
P.O. 7004, Troy, Michigan 48007
In Canada: Box 1717, Postal Station A
Windsor, Ontario N9A 6Y1

ISBN 1-884137-78-4

CONTENTS

1 Living in the Light 5

2 I Remember Israel 11

3 Trust Daddy and Jump! 19

4 Competing for the Gold 27

5 I'm Looking . . . But Which Way? 35

6 Listen — He Speaks Ever So Softly 41

7 Somebody's Children 51

8 Who Is Mary? 57

9 Eat, Drink and Be Merry 65

10 Just Say, "Thank You!" 73

11 Go Home a Winner 83

12 You Are God's Gift to a Lost World 91

13 A Blaze of Glory 95

14 Is There Room in Your Heart for Him? 101

Chapter 1

Living in the Light

An artist sat at his easel creating a gripping, powerful painting. Using dark, somber hues, he drew dreary, empty fields framed by stark, skeleton-like trees, under a cold, snow-laden sky.

In one corner of the canvas he sketched a lonely, desolate house, its stark lines fading into the shadows of the night. Then the artist paused to contemplate the bleak and melancholy scene he had created. After a few moments, he picked up his brush to add a finishing touch.

With a dab of bright yellow paint, he put a

warm, glowing light in the window of the house. And suddenly, magically, the whole scene was transformed — that single light overcame all the darkness and spoke of hope and life!

This story reminds me of the impact the birth of Jesus made on the world and the entire history of mankind. As the Apostle John declared, *In Him was life; and the life was the light of men* (John 1:4).

The light in the sky

For 400 years before the birth of Jesus there had been no new Word from God, no prophetic voice, no new revelations. Man's attempts to control his own destiny had brought confusion and disaster. The shadows of sin and hopelessness had settled over the land of Israel, and the whole world had sunk into the dismal depths of unbridled sinfulness and despair.

Then, with a stroke of God's hand, He brightened the landscape of history and gave hope again to a dreary world. He put a light in the sky! The star of Christmas lit up the sky and captured the attention of all men in all nations.

Why a star? Why a light? The Almighty could just as easily have spoken to mankind as He did to the shepherds through the choir of heavenly angels. Why was such a momentous event as the birth of Jesus marked first by a light in the sky?

I believe it was because when God flung back the curtains of heaven and opened His throne room directly to earth ... light poured through as the Son of God made His entrance into the world.

The earth was dreary, dark, and lonely. But with a single stroke, God changed the picture — He put a light in the window.

The light in the stable

In Rembrandt's famous painting of the nativity scene, all the light in the stable is centered around the Christ child. This is a fitting depiction, for He is the Source of all light.

It is no accident that the Son of God came to a stable rather than a palace. He came, not just to the rich, the privileged, the powerful alone, but to all men — even the poorest and most humble.

Yet, the wealthy were not excluded from His presence. Those Wise Men who sought Him were obviously men of means, since they brought rich gifts of gold and precious spices. When they sought Him, humbling themselves to come where He was, they, too, were welcomed.

Jesus said, *I am come a light into the world, that whosoever believeth on me should not abide in darkness* (John 12:46).

The shepherds were the first to arrive on the

scene (see Luke 2:8-20; Matthew 2:11). Sometime later there came the "kings," or magi, from afar. Have you ever wondered why they all didn't arrive at the same time to worship Christ?

I'm told there is a prophetic significance to the timing of those events — that Christ came to the Jews first, then to the Gentiles.

But all who came to find the Source of light in the stable were received joyfully.

The light in our hearts

Today there is no single brilliant star lighting up the sky. Nor do pilgrims to Bethlehem find a divine light still emanating from the place where once a rude stable stood.

Where, then, is the light of the world? It still burns ... in the hearts of those who believe in Jesus Christ and who receive Him as their Lord and Savior. We are His luminaries in today's world. If the people around us are to see the light of Christ, they must see it in you and me!

We ourselves don't have the ability to be lights — but we can be reflectors of the Light. When we allow Christ's light to come inside our hearts, the Holy Spirit, the transformer, makes us lamps through which the light shines.

God, through the Holy Spirit, transforms the stable of men's hearts into the temple of glory!

The same Jesus who said, *I am the light of the world* (John 8:12) also says to us, *Ye are the light of the world* (Matthew 5:14). And we are to let our light — His light — shine forth.

He said, *If I be lifted up from earth,* [I] *will draw all men unto me* (John 12:32). As we allow Christ to be lifted up in our lives, He'll do the illuminating. He'll attract others to Himself.

How often have you met a person who had such a glow around him that you knew he was a child of God even before you were introduced to him? There is a kind of peace and tranquility, a love that just radiates to others. And people are drawn to such a person because it is natural to be drawn to light.

In the neighborhood where Jack and I used to live, the people on our block all decided to put out luminaries as decorations at Christmas time. A luminary is a simple brown paper bag filled with enough sand to keep it from blowing away . . . with a small candle inside.

A single candle didn't give off much light by itself, but when the whole street was lined with these luminaries, the whole neighborhood was bathed in a soft, beautiful glow!

One of the ongoing themes of this ministry is "Lighting New Fires of Revival, Redemption, and Reconciliation" through our outreaches. And I believe the way to kindle those anew in the New Year is to allow the light of the Lord to shine through each of us.

I'm not talking about the fires of fanaticism that break out of control and wreak havoc and destruction wherever they go. Instead, I'm talking about the glow, that divine light that softly shines through and combines with the light shining from other believers about us.

We must be faithful. We must not fail. A world dying in darkness is looking for the Light.

In the words of the familiar chorus:
This little light of mine,
I'm gonna let it shine,
Let it shine,
Let it shine,
Let it shine!

Chapter 2

I Remember Israel

I shall never forget the first time I saw Israel! There I was, newly married and already traveling to the land I had learned to love as a little girl in Sunday school.

Israel wasn't modern then. I remember thinking that the land looked just as it must have in ancient times. Yet, it seemed to me to be almost a bridge . . . between the past and the future.

Surely, Israel is the most exciting nation in the world. Its very existence seems to culminate all Bible prophecy. My husband has often remarked that Israel is the key to all

Bible prophecy.

I Remember My First Impression of Israel!

Wandering through the narrow streets of Jerusalem during my first visit, everything I saw and experienced seemed so far removed from modern times! In fact, some of the shops I entered seemed to be just as they were 2,000 years ago.

My first impression of Israel, however, was not just of a land rich in ancient history, but a land that had been stripped and starved.

Not too many years prior to my first pilgrimage, Jews from all points of the globe had begun to flood back into their homeland, fulfilling ancient prophecies with their arrival. As a people, the Jews had been persecuted, beaten, and deprived. Many were survivors of Hitler's horrible death camps, having lost their entire families as well as all earthly possessions to the atrocities of Nazism during World War II.

Thousands of Jewish refugees arrived in Israel with literally nothing more than the clothes on their backs . . . and a fierce determination to make their Israel bloom!

I Remember the Diversity of Israel!

When Jack and I returned to Israel a few years later, I was truly amazed! Israel had undergone an almost unbelievable transformation! I could see the fulfillment of Isaiah 35:1 . . . *the desert shall rejoice, and blossom as the rose.*

The Jews, with their innovative genius, had installed irrigation systems throughout their entire land . . . instantly transforming arid deserts into fruitful, productive orchards and gardens. *And the desolate land shall be tilled, whereas it lay desolate in the sight of all that passed by. And they shall say, This land that was desolate is become like the garden of Eden* (Ezekiel 36:34, 35). I witnessed this!

Construction in the cities had also begun to move forward, and amid the treasured antiquities were now high-rise buildings with every modern convenience.

Throughout the land, I was struck with the diversity I saw everywhere! It was not unusual to see a man leading a little donkey loaded down with burdens alongside a busy street teeming with trucks and cars. Nor was it unusual to see a supersonic jet roar over the head of an Arab riding a camel.

I discovered that in this incredibly diverse 20th century Israel, I could:
- Visit Qumran, where the Dead Sea scrolls were discovered . . . or tour the Department of Nuclear Physics at the Weizman Institute.
- Experience the coolness of the mountains and pastures of Galilee . . . and the parched deserts of the southern region near the

Dead Sea.
- Learn about the rich heritage of the Jewish culture . . . discover more about the Arabs and their predominant religion, Islam . . . and also worship Jesus with other Christians.

I Remember the Sights of Israel!

Today, as I reminisce about Israel, I can still see the fishermen casting their nets into the Sea of Galilee . . . the shepherds caring for their flocks in the fields . . . the barren desert where Jesus endured the devil's temptations . . .

I can envision modern Jerusalem, with the ancient wonders of old Jerusalem entwined within it . . . the Jews praying at their Wailing Wall . . . the tomb of Lazarus . . . the field of Boaz, where Ruth and Naomi gleaned wheat and where the shepherds later received the angel's message of the Messiah's birth . . .

I remember the Garden of Gethsemane, where Jesus' sweat was as drops of blood . . . and Golgotha, where He suffered the shame and the agony of the sum of mankind's sins.

Of all the places we visited, I can say that the Garden of the Resurrection, where our Lord first revealed himself as risen from the dead, was the most profound place for me! In fact, I was moved to tears as I sat quietly, just praying.

I recall the awesomeness of the Valley of Megiddo, or Jezreel, where the battle of all battles — ARMAGEDDON — will take place. It's such a vast, open area, and a place of such prophetic destiny.

As we winded our way through the teeming streets of Tel Aviv, I could not help but realize: "This land means EVERYTHING to the Jews!"

For them, Israel is their home, their life, their honor, and their purpose. Apart from Israel, the Jew believes he hardly has an existence.

I Remember the People!

I have many fond memories of the Jewish people!

My husband and I taped many television specials and programs there. Many people opened their hearts and homes to us! They knew we were Christians, but they could also sense that we loved THEM! Jack and I were even welcomed to tape inside the Jewish Knessett building! The members I interviewed were so very kind and gracious!

I remember the openness of Israel's President Yitzhak Navon. He was such a magnetic personality, and will always live in my memory as one of the most genuine, kind men I have ever met. He knew his Old Testament thoroughly and easily conversed with Jack about Bible prophecies. We were invited to his private residence, where he and Jack discussed the Bible, end-time events, and the role of Israel in the last days.

On another occasion, we were invited to dinner at the home of the late Prime Minister Menachem Begin. The dinner, however, was canceled suddenly — due to the assassination of Egypt's President Anwar Sadat! Prime Minister Begin had to leave immediately for Tel Aviv and an emergency meeting of his cabinet — so I did not get to interview him after dinner, as planned.

I was fortunate to interview Abba Eban, former Israeli Ambassador to the United Nations who was often called "the Voice of Israel." And I met and interviewed Moshe Arens, who then was Israel's Ambassador to the United States.

I also remember the beautiful, innocent children. On one of my videos, I taped songs with a group of them. They sat on my lap, we talked, we laughed and played together. When I think of the war that has gone on constantly there, and when I think of what the Jews as a people have gone through, it tears at my heart.

The Jews of Israel are only a heartbeat away from disaster!

I have a very dear friend — Estee Levine — with whom I have corresponded regularly for many years. Her residence is in Jerusalem, and she is responsible for preparing the accommodations for thousands of tourists who visit Israel each year.

During the Desert Storm operation, Israel

was frequently under attack by Saddam Hussein's air raids. During those war-torn months, Estee wrote me about the birth of her granddaughter. She wrote: "We had time of great rejoicing! And we could rejoice — even in the midst of rocket attacks!"

I've always found that kind of optimism among the Israelis — even among the children. They have such a valiant attitude of spirit!

It's as if God has instilled His own optimism into His people, because they are ultimately going to win. Micah 4:3 says, *And they shall beat their swords into plowshares, and their spears into pruninghooks: nation shall not lift up a sword against nation, neither shall they learn war any more.* That day of peace is coming!

I Remember Jesus!

Seeing the places where He walked, recalling the events of His life, even receiving communion in the place of His Resurrection made me feel so much closer to Jesus!

Time and again, Jack and I found ourselves retracing the steps of Jesus and the disciples. There was Capernaum, where we explored fascinating ruins and again traced the steps of Jesus, who taught the multitudes there. I almost expected to see the throngs described in the Bible, pressing closer and closer in, to hear the words of life! When we walked along the

Via Dolorosa, we could not help but painfully recall Christ's final steps before Calvary.

We served communion to those of our tour group in that quiet garden, and I was emotionally stirred by the experience! I shall never forget that from where I was sitting, I could look up . . . to see Golgotha, the place of the skull, where His crucifixion took place . . . and I could also look down . . . at the stone which had been rolled away from the tomb that could not hold Him. What a powerful contrast!

Experiencing Israel in all her diversity and splendor has added more depth and dimension to my faith, and has given me many wonderful memories.

Chapter 3

Trust Daddy and Jump!

It's amazing how often I am awakened in the middle of the night and find myself thanking and praising God for all of His grace, mercy and blessings. Recently, I have found myself, in that quiet time of the early morning, reminiscing about my happy childhood. How very grateful I am to the Lord for such beautiful memories. I remember with fondness and joy the good times we had together as a family. My father was a big man — well over six feet tall, fun-loving and tender — and my brothers were the best companions a little girl could have. My precious, sweet

Mother, though petite, had robust energy and always joined in our many outings of picnics, concerts, boating, swimming and a multitude of events conducted by our church.

We had a favorite place to go in the summer for swimming. Since we lived in Michigan, where there were various areas one could enjoy for this fun-time sport, my father taught me to swim at a very early age. I must have been about seven when I had my first experience at diving. The place we liked the best had a twenty, perhaps even a thirty-foot high waterfall. My older brother was a wonderful swimmer and I'd watch in awe as he made his way to the top of the waterfall and then dove off. I wondered if I'd ever be able to do that. I hoped so, but it did look scary.

The day came when my Dad said, "Rexella, go on up there and jump off. I'll be here to get you." At first I paused, looked at him to make certain I'd heard correctly, and he nodded his head and urged me on. Self-assured, I strutted off and made my way to the top. But when I got there, I said to my brother who had followed me, "I can't do it."

"Sure you can," he confidently coaxed, "you're a great little swimmer. I know you can do it. You just trust Daddy and jump."

From the top of the falls I looked over to the side bank where my mother and little brother were waiting and watching for me to do my first jump. "I can't disappoint my family," I thought. "You go first," I said to Bob, still hesitant. Then I looked down and my Father called up, "Jump, I'll be right here for you." I saw his smiling face and remembered that he had never failed me in the past. So I took my first leap of faith and trust.

The first thing I remember was hitting the water with a thud and sinking down, down, down. All of a sudden I felt the strength of my Daddy's hands as he pulled me up to the top. What a relief and how good it felt to have his hands gripping mine. I clung to his neck for a moment and was rewarded with his words, "Good girl! I knew you could do it."

This was the first illustration of trust that I can really remember and to which I relate when I think about trust and all that it means. The word trust implies reliance on someone or something. It calls to mind other words such as confidence, faith, dependence, assurance and certainty. Good words.

We know love is freely given, but trust is something that must be earned. You can look at someone and think, "I love him or her for Jesus' sake," but you can't trust them until you know them and are assured that they have earned the right to be trusted. In particular, in the cultural climate in which we find ourselves today, we have come to realize that one just can't trust everybody. That's a sad commentary, but true.

But there is Someone who is fully

trustworthy — worthy that is, of our total trust. That Someone is Jesus. We can take Him at His Word, and that Word is the Bible.

It isn't always easy to trust. The apostle Peter discovered this when he jumped into the raging sea to go to Jesus who was walking on the water. Remember the story in Matthew 14:22-33? As long as Peter kept his eyes on Jesus, trusting Him, he was fine as he actually walked on the water; but when Peter continued walking against the boisterous wind; he was afraid, and began to sink. It isn't always easy to step out from that which is secure into something precarious. Nor is it easy to keep trusting when the waves of fear and doubt overwhelm us. Let's never forget this beautiful thought when we reach out to Jesus: His hand will always be there to save us, guide us and help us. When Jesus reached out His hand to Peter and caught him, Peter was safe.

Trust Him With Your Past

First of all, we can trust Him with our past. I John 1:7 assures us if we walk in the light, as He Himself is in the light, we have fellowship one with another, and the blood of Jesus Christ His Son, cleanseth us from all sin. When it says all, it means all — all of the past. We can trust Him for cleansing, for obliterating all that would otherwise stand between us and our holy God.

Psalm 103:12 tells us, *As far as the east is from the west, so far hath he removed our transgressions from us.* And that's a long, long way. Who can measure it? I was reminded recently that the distance between the North and South Pole is measurable because there is a limit to northness and southness. However, there is no East Pole or West Pole. Isn't it amazing that the Bible is explicit in saying *As far as the east is from the west . . .* I find that awesome. To think that's how God removes our sin from us. Yes, immeasurably! When God deals with our sin, a radical removal takes place. What a wonderful, trustworthy God we have!

Hebrews 8:10 provides assurance of this truth with these words: *For I will be merciful to their unrighteousness, and their sins and their iniquities will I remember no more.* It's as if we had never sinned or done anything wrong or displeasing to God. How amazing to think we can trust God with our past.

Trust Him With the Future

Then, we can trust God with the future. Those familiar words in Proverbs 3 take on new meaning as one thinks about the implications of the word trust: *Trust in the Lord with all thine heart; and lean not unto thine own understanding. In all thy ways acknowledge him, and he shall direct thy paths* (vv.5,6).

That word "shall" in this verse speaks of the future. It says we can trust Him to guide us in the days to come. How does He do this? He does it in different ways. Let's consider three: 1. Through prayer. 2. Through circumstances. 3. Through the certainty of His Word.

First of all He has promised to be trustworthy as we pray. How very often we sense the strength of our Lord as we ask Him to bless and guide us in prayer. He alone can change situations beyond our control. Without reservation we are assured that He can be trusted to care for each and every request. Sometimes His answer may be, "wait," sometimes He says, "This is not good for you," and sometimes he says, "Yes, it is accomplished." Have you experienced the peace of knowing that you have been heard even before you arise from your knees? Remember the words of Isaiah in chapter 65, verse 24: *And it shall come to pass, that before they call, I will answer; and while they are yet speaking, I will hear.*

Let's also consider how God guides us through circumstances. Remember the Old Testament story of Ruth? What a beautiful picture of what it means to trust in God. In this book we read how Ruth decided to stay with her mother-in-law, Naomi, after tragedy struck her family. God blessed Ruth for her faithfulness in the form of a good husband, Boaz, and a child (from whom King David was a direct descendant). Had Ruth not listened to the voice of the Lord and followed her Mother-In-Law to Israel, God could not have used circumstances to lead her to Boaz and bless her with such a sweet reward. What a beautiful commitment Ruth 2:12 reveals: *The Lord recompense thy work, and a full reward be given thee of the Lord God of Israel, under whose wings thou art come to trust.* Oh, that we might all follow the guidance of the Lord so that He might use circumstances in our lives to bless us and reward us with heaven's best.

Lastly, let us think about how God guides us through His Word. The Bible is not a lottery system whereby we choose a verse of scripture for each day and end up taking just what we want to hear. But it is a book of
- "instruction and correction," II Timothy 3:16, 17
- "guidance," Psalm 119:105
- "assurance and peace in a troubled world," Isaiah 26:3.

I could list an entire page of what the Bible can be trusted to do for us, but let me just assure you, it will never fail, it will never change and it will always be relevant to our daily life.

Often, as I have my devotions with the Lord, I ask Him to make my mind and heart receptive to what He wants to reveal to me through His Word. As I continue to read and meditate, there it is — just what I need. I love Psalm 119:140, *Thy word is very pure: therefore thy servant loveth it.*

The world is not a safe place. Everyone is talking about violence. A Dallas newspaper front-page article says that guns soon may pass vehicles as a top killer, according to federal health officials. Already, shootings cause more deaths than traffic accidents in Texas, six other states and the District of Columbia. This find came as public opinion polls showed growing public alarm about violent crime. Let's hear the words of David when he said: *The Lord is my rock; and my fortress, and my deliverer, The God of my rock; in him will I trust; he is my Shield and the horn of my salvation, my high tower, and my refuge, my savior; thou savest me from violence* (II Samuel 22:2, 3).

There is only one place where we can go and be assured that placing our trust will not be misplaced dependence, and that is at the feet of Jesus. My brother's words come back to me with true meaning for today's stress-filled world, "Trust Daddy and jump!" Do you know the joy of trusting your heavenly Father? He stands ready to catch you as you take that leap of faith and — jump!

Chapter 4

Competing for the Gold

During the winter Olympics in Lillehammer, Norway, the finest athletes from all over the world gathered to compete in various sports events. Jack and I were especially interested in the skiing and skating competitions, and watched in awe as both men and women set new world records.

What a thrill to see these champions receive the victor's reward and be presented with the Olympic Gold Medal with the great crowds in the stands looking on, and the television cameras providing international coverage; the whole world was watching!

Most of us could never compete in a world class sports competition like the Olympics, but as Christians, we are faced with the challenge of running a race for the Lord. The whole world is watching to see how we run the race — will we be champions or defeated competitors?

The Apostle Paul had visited Greece where the first Olympic Games were held centuries ago. No doubt he was thinking of the comparison between Christians and Olympians when he wrote. *Know ye not that they which run in a race run all, but one receiveth the prize? So run, that ye may obtain. And every one that striveth for the mastery is temperate in all things. Now they do it to obtain a corruptible crown: but we an incorruptible. I therefore so run, not as uncertainly; so fight I, not as one that beateth the air: but I keep under my body and bring it into subjection: lest that by any means, when I have preached to others, I myself should be a castaway* (I Corinthians 9:24-47).

Dedication and Commitment

In order to be a winner, a competitor must meet certain prerequisites and prepare his body for the race. No one is born a Gold Medal Olympian.

Athletes train and condition their bodies to compete. They are temperate, or moderate, in all things. They watch their diet, engage in challenging, strength-building exercise, and get proper rest.

The apostle says, "If they do this to gain a corruptible crown, a reward that will pass away, how much more should we be dedicated and committed to winning an incorruptible, eternal reward."

What does it mean to be temperate in all things? We are to have pure lives! We are to keep ourselves from contamination.

One of the saddest moments of the Olympics in Lillehammer was when one of the athletes was disqualified after tests revealed illegal drugs in his blood. He went home in shame and disgrace.

Paul warns that the same thing can happen to us, but with far greater consequences. He said he continuously worked to keep his body pure and under subjection. Paul was saying that he did not want to run the race, then be disqualified. I keep checking up on my personal dedication and commitment, he said, lest that by any means, when I have preached to others, I myself should be a castaway.

I'm sure you know of Christians who failed to be temperate in all things . . . who did not keep their lives pure. Perhaps they dropped out of the race altogether, or sadly faced the humiliation of being publicly disqualified.

I heard a report about a group of ministers that came from all across the nation to attend a convention at a major hotel. After the meeting was over, the hotel management said that 75 percent of the rooms occupied by these preachers requested X- and R-rated movies.

Turn Loose of Hindrances

God help us to keep our lives pure. *Wherefore seeing we also are compassed about with so great a cloud of witnesses, let us lay aside every weight, and the sin which doth so easily beset us* (Hebrews 12:1).

Let's lay aside "every weight" — we can't be just partially pure, you see. We must lay everything aside. The writer goes on to say, "and the sin which doth so easily beset us." I'm fully convinced that each of us has a tendency toward something that could cause us to fall. The passage doesn't say "sins," but the one particular thing that so easily gets to you. You know what it is in your life — I know what it is in mine.

We need to examine ourselves to know where our weaknesses lie so that we can defend ourselves against the devil's temptations.

I was reading a devotional book about a woman who was extremely obese and was having a real struggle losing weight. (She may have been like the person who said temptation never bothered him because when it came around, he succumbed.)

As this lady was praying, she said, "Lord, You see what a problem I'm having. Why don't You just take away my appetite?"

And the Lord answered, "If I did, what

would you have to do?"

You can keep yourself under control. You can avoid things you know are hindrances to victorious living. You can lay aside the weights that slow you down . . . the temptations that are your greatest weaknesses. God will protect you from the evil one. He will not protect you from yourself!

Patience to Endure

Let us run with patience the race that is set before us (Hebrews 12:1).

Everyone in the race can look like a champion at the starting line. But that's not where it counts! The winner is determined at the end of the course!

It's not enough to start strong. We must be patient . . . and have endurance. I noticed in the Olympics that particularly in the long races, the winner often was not the runner who started off in front. Sometimes the winner didn't make his move to the front until the final lap.

Patience and endurance are just as important to a successful Christian life as the dedication and commitment one has at the start.

At the end of his life, the Apostle Paul could say, *I have fought a good fight, I have finished my course, I have kept the faith: Henceforth there is laid up for me a crown of righteousness, which the Lord, the righteous judge, shall give me at that day* (11 Timothy 4:7,8).

Keep Your Eyes on the Goal

As I watched the Olympic contest I noticed that no one ever turned to look at anything or anybody else — they kept their eyes on the goal. If someone fell beside them, they kept moving. If another athlete came near them, they kept their eyes straight ahead.

I love what Hebrews 12:2 says — *Looking unto Jesus.* Even though it's a continued thought, this statement is part of the verse before it that talks about laying aside weights and sin, and running with patience. While you're doing this, the apostle says, keep your eyes on the goal. LOOK UNTO JESUS!

There are many distractions in the world. There are discouragements, especially when we get weary, and when we see other Christians failing and falling out of the race.

But if we look unto Jesus, He will help us stay in the race. If we keep our eyes on the goal, we can make it to the end. If we keep our eyes on the Lord, it matters not what others do.

I hope you'll join Dr. Van Impe and me in a new resolve to run a better race for the Lord. There is a reward for those who finish the course . . . and you can be a winner. "So run, that ye may obtain." The Lord has a very special race for each of us to run. You know what your challenge is.

So we must be built up in the faith and ready for the challenge ahead of us. I'm excited about being in the race and . . . competing for the gold.

Chapter 5

I'm Looking . . . But Which Way?

What is the first thing you notice about a person? Some would say the color of their hair, their stature or even their weight. I must admit that I am immediately drawn to the eyes. Perhaps this is why I like the statement, "The eye is the window of the soul." It was Benjamin Franklin who related this good thought, "Learn to be gracious with the eyes; look deep into their eyes, and say with your eyes, 'I like you.'"

I especially enjoy looking into the eyes of children. Often I find myself wanting to get down to their level since they, above all, have that gentle, yet intense and honest way of looking directly into our eyes. They have discovered a secret which sometimes gets lost as they move into adulthood — it is this, the eyes reveal so much. Perhaps it's the child in me, but conversation seems more personal when I am able to look into the eyes of the one with whom I am conversing. There seems to be an openness in communication when we can express our thoughts through our eyes as well as by our words.

The eyes also can be a barometer revealing the state of our health. Doctors, for instance, look into the eyes when one is sick, and ophthalmologists detect many bodily illnesses the same way. The Bible has much to say about the eyes. The writer of Proverbs speaks of the bloodshot eyes of those who drink (Proverbs 23:28, 29). In fact, there are 499 references to eyes, and 98 to the eye in God's Word. Since God has given such prominence and importance to the eye gate, Satan, with all of his sly and cunning ways brought sin into the world by persuading Eve to look and then partake of the forbidden fruit (Gen. 3:5-7).

God often speaks of His own eyes. How comforting it is to know that His eyes are lovingly upon us. *For the eyes of the Lord run to and fro throughout the whole earth, to show himself strong in the behalf of them whose heart is perfect toward him* (2 Chronicles 16:9 — also notice Deuteronomy 11:12; Job 34:21;

and Psalm 33:18).

Why are our eyes so important? It is because what we see goes into our emotions (the soul). The light of the soul is what gives understanding, sound judgment, and the ability to discern between good and evil, truth and falsehood. Jesus spoke of this: *The light of the body is the eye; therefore when thine eye is single* (a clear conscience), *thy whole body is full of light; but when thine eye is evil, thy body also is full of darkness. Take heed therefore that the light which is in thee be not darkness* (Luke 11:34, 35).

Walking Visuals

What do others see when looking at us? If they are to be rightly influenced, how important it is that what they see is God-like. We are walking visuals. The Apostle Paul cautioned that we should be careful how we walk, *not as unwise, but as wise, redeeming the time because the days are evil* (Ephesians 5:15, 16).

I heard the story of a little girl who told her pastor she knew Jesus and was saved. "Which one of my sermons brought you to Christ?" he asked. "It wasn't your preaching, it was my aunt's practicing," she responded.

Indeed! What we do and say is being noticed. *Man looketh on the outward appearance* (I Samuel 16:7). That's why we are to *let our light so shine before mankind, that they may see our good works, and glorify our Father which is in heaven* (Matt. 5:16).

On one occasion, when the Apostle Paul was accused of being a troublemaker, stirring up riots among the Jews and a ringleader of the "Nazarene sect," he stood before his accusers and Governor Felix saying, "I strive to always have a conscience without offense toward God and man" (see Acts 24:16). What a wonderful way to live!

With all the discouraging news in the world today, seeming inconsistencies in the lives of those around us, and despair on the faces of millions of people, which way can we look to find peace and satisfaction?

Three Different Directions

We can look in three different directions: (1) Backward, to be discouraged; (2) outward, to be disheartened; and (3) upward, to be delighted.

Backwards:

More often than not, looking back leads to defeat and discouragement and possibly self destruction like Lot's wife. We have a good biblical example in the Apostle Paul, who said, *Forgetting those things which are behind, and reaching forth unto those things which are before, I press toward the mark for the prize of the high calling of God in Christ Jesus* (Philippians 3:13, 14).

God can be counted on to give a silver lining to our dark clouds if we'll begin looking forward. A friend has written: "Let your life be a statement, more than your words, that Someone else is in charge. Let your demeanor reflect quality inner control, stability that comes from knowing and accepting that God is in charge. In God's perfect timing wrongs will be righted, circumstances will change, He will come to your rescue. To believe this is to move ahead and live with hope."

I have been asked, "How do you forget the bad times, the hurts, the injustices?" My response is that we can't blot out the past, but forgetting means not allowing the past to affect the present.

We can put whatever has hurt us under the blood of Christ. We can forget by imitating the way Christ forgives us — just as if it never occurred (Hebrews 8:12).

Outward:

As one looks around at the world today, he or she could become disheartened and disillusioned. The world is in a mess. Just pick up the newspaper, or turn on the evening news and it's enough to disturb any thinking person.

How do we avoid the disillusionment and anxiety? David the psalmist said, *It will not fasten its grip on me* (see Psalm 101:3). There you have it; don't allow it to grasp hold of your thinking.

What does God say? He tells us to cast our burdens on Christ (I Peter 5:7). We are human and feel concern, but we can turn it over to Him saying, "God, this is too big for me to handle." By keeping our eyes on Jesus and the eternal truths of God's word, we will be focusing our attention on that which enables us to handle all the bad things happening around us (see Hebrews 12:2).

Upward:

Remember what David the psalmist said? *I will lift up mine eyes unto the hills, from whence cometh my help* (Psalm 121:1). This is surely the only direction to look for help, comfort, and yes, for delight in our souls and lives. We can bring our thirsty and wilting minds and bodies to the everlasting well of water, Jesus Christ Himself (John 4). All He asks is that we keep looking up, and as we do, look forward to an eternity with Him. Let us pray this beautiful prayer of the psalmist, *I will direct my prayer unto thee, and will look up* (Psalm 5:3).

*I WILL LIFT UP MINE EYES
UNTO THE HILLS . . .*
— Psalm 121:1

Chapter 6

Listen — He Speaks Ever So Softly

It was long past time for my annual physical, in fact, I was enjoying such good health and vitality that it had been three years since I had visited my doctor. However, at the conclusion of a thorough exam, the report was quite disconcerting. (Before I proceed, let me encourage all of my readers, if at all possible to go for that annual "check-up.")

"We will have to do some tests," the doctor explained, "then, in a couple of weeks, we will know where we stand."

Immediately, my mind was filled with different thoughts. "Can this be me who is experiencing this questionable report? No! My doctor is wrong! What if she is not?" By the time I got home and shared the news with Jack I found myself asking God, "What's this all about?"

In compliance with the doctor, I took the medical tests and began the long wait for the results. All the while, we were praying and seeking the Lord for His divine purpose and will to be accomplished in my life.

By the end of the two weeks, we found ourselves rejoicing in the faithfulness of God. I knew He had everything under control. Deep in my heart, I knew it would be all right. "But Lord," I asked, "what is the purpose behind this trial?"

Then — the night before we received the results of my tests — Jack looked over at me and said, "I have peace in this matter, so tonight let's go out and celebrate this victory in our lives!"

We went to a lovely restaurant that is meant for celebrating and fine dining. A nice, handsome pianist softly played the piano in the corner of the dining room, and candles softly lit each of the tables. Jack and I laughed, enjoyed our luscious dinner and shared in a wonderful conversation about the Lord. It was an evening I'll never forget.

As we prepared to leave, I expressed to my

husband how much I wanted to go and thank the pianist for sharing his special talent with us. Being musicians ourselves we were impressed with his tremendous ability to "tickle the ivories."

"You have a beautiful touch on the keyboard," I told him.

"Thank you," he answered. "I am sorry if you saw me staring at you and your husband." He explained: "For a year, my fiancée and I watched your television program faithfully. She used your ministry to help lead me to the Lord, and then . . . she died. She was only 38 years old and I have been bitter toward the Lord and unable to pray ever since."

I reached out and took his hand from the keyboard and stated: "God doesn't want you to be bitter and neither does she. Your fiancée is in a better place right now and you will be with her again — perhaps soon. The best thing you could do right now is to get your heart right with the Lord, so that when He comes again, you can go and be at her side."

Jack, who has always been sensitive to the moving of the Holy Spirit, began to explain to this young man the Scriptures and how *it is appointed unto men once to die* (Hebrews 9:27). Then he added, "Your sweetheart is in heaven and awaits your homecoming. Be ready, Brian!"

Jack and I were so blessed as we watched the Lord begin to move in his heart. Right at the piano, with tears streaming down his face he recommitted his life to the Lord Jesus Christ. He looked up at both of us and said, "I can hardly wait to call my fiancée's twin sister to tell her what has happened tonight." We had a word of prayer and promised to send him our video about heaven.

The next morning, I heard from my doctor. My tests showed that I was just fine. The doctor said, "You and Jack go out and celebrate, Rexella." She did not know that we had already claimed the good report and the special blessing we had found in doing so. Of course, we continue to rejoice and thank the Lord for the results of the test, but we realize that if for no other reason we had gone through this trial, Jack and I could be at the restaurant that night to speak to the young pianist.

God's ways are so much greater than ours. This was probably the Lord's plan all along! How important it is for you and me as Christians today to listen to the Holy Spirit and obey His leading in our lives! The things and events that surround us are real and at times they can be overwhelming, and we are unable to recognize Jesus and the guidance of His Spirit. Let the circumstances be what they may. Always maintain complete reliance upon Him and listen to the often quiet voice of His Spirit as He leads you into victory and blessings yet to come. Be totally unrestraining, be willing to risk everything. We do not know when His voice will come again, so be ever-aware and obey.

I realized, there are three very important lessons in regard to listening to the Holy Spirit that we can learn from this personal experience with the young man.

1. We must listen when the Holy Spirit is leading us.

I Thessalonians 5:19, says: *Quench not the Spirit.* That means, when you are being led by the Holy Spirit, you must listen to His voice. The little promptings and opportunities that God passes along your way mean you must be faithful. Follow the Lord's leading in these situations so that you do not quench His ministry in your life.

In Acts the 8th chapter, we read the wonderful testimony of Philip the evangelist as he was led to a desert road that descends from Jerusalem to Gaza. Once there, *the Spirit said unto Philip, Go near, and join thyself to this Chariot* (Acts 8:29). Arriving at the chariot, there was an Ethiopian eunuch, a court official, who was reading the book of Isaiah. However, he did not grasp what the prophet was saying, so beginning with the passage of Scripture in Isaiah, Philip led the Ethiopian eunuch to a relationship with Jesus Christ.

If Philip had not obeyed the prompting of the Holy Spirit in his life — and, if Philip had not preached Jesus to the Ethiopian eunuch —

this court official may never have been won to the Lord.

The same was true for Jack and me as we talked with this young pianist that night. If we had just walked out, not wanting to get involved, or if we had talked with the musician about his fine musical skills and not talked about the Lord or the Scriptures, this young man may never have received the ministry he so desperately needed.

2. When the Holy Spirit guides us, He will empower us to do His will.

A beautiful example of this dynamic thought can be found in the life of the Apostle Peter.

Previous to Peter being filled with the Holy Spirit, he was a spiritually weak man. Who can forget the night when Jesus was brought before Caiaphas the high priest, and the scribes and the elders? Peter lingered outside in the courtyard where he was confronted by a servant girl who asked if he was one of Jesus' disciples. Peter vehemently denied the Lord three times that night.

Remember, this was before the Holy Spirit filled Peter's life.

Oh, the grace of God! Only 50 days after the denial, we read the wonderful account in Acts, chapter 2, of Peter's boldness on the Day of Pentecost. This was the event Jesus prophesied before he ascended: *But ye shall receive power, after that the Holy Ghost is come upon you: and ye shall be witnesses unto me both in Jerusalem, and in all Judea, and in Samaria, and unto the uttermost parts of the earth* (Acts 1:8).

After Peter was filled with the Holy Spirit, he stood up before the crowd that day — unashamed and unafraid — proclaiming the Good News of Jesus Christ. Three thousand souls were won to the Lord!

Soon after this, Peter and John were brought before the Sadducees who commanded that Peter and John no longer teach in the name of Jesus (see Acts 4:13). But Peter would not be intimidated. He said (along with the Apostle John), *Whether it be right in the sight of God to hearken unto you more than unto God, judge ye. For we cannot but speak the things which we have seen and heard* (Acts 4:19,20).

Scripture also records: *With great power gave the apostles witness of the resurrection of the Lord Jesus: and great grace was upon them all* (Acts 4:33).

What made this difference in the life of the Apostle Peter? It was the Person of the Holy Spirit.

Previous to being filled with the Holy Spirit, Peter was so weak, in and of himself, he denied Christ in front of a damsel. After the infilling of the Holy Spirit, Peter became bold in faith and proclaimed the Gospel in the face of beatings and eventually, martyrdom (he was crucified upside down).

3. When the Holy Spirit leads and empowers us for the sake of the Gospel, and we faithfully obey His promptings — not quenching the Holy Spirit . . . then blessing comes!

That evening, after Jack and I shared in this precious conversation with our young pianist, we walked away rejoicing. We were happy about the wonderful things God did in that man's life — and in ours — by bringing us all together for this special moment of ministry. We felt truly blessed! Winning souls and witnessing for Christ always produces joy.

For what is our hope, or joy, or crown of rejoicing? Are not even ye in the presence of our Lord Jesus Christ at his coming? For ye are our glory and joy (I Thessalonians 2:19, 20).

Jack and I have often found that in attempting to bless others, we are also blessed. As we attempt to reach out and water the lives of others with Scripture, we are watered ourselves. As we comfort others, our own comfort is increased. We find consolation and gladness in our own lives as we give to others.

Jesus said, *Give, and it shall be given unto you; good measure, pressed down, and shaken together, and running over, shall men give into your bosom. For with the same measure that ye mete withal it shall be measured to you again* (Luke 6:38).

Proverbs says it this way: *The liberal souls*

shall be made fat: and he that watereth shall be watered also himself (Proverbs 11:25).

We must remember: *Whosoever will save his life shall lose it; but whosoever shall lose his life for my sake and the gospel's, the same shall save it* (Mark 8:35). True life is found as you give yours away in service to others.

In closing, I am reminded of the Dead Sea, located between Israel and the Jordan, whose water content is so salty that very little is able to exist within its waters.

The intrinsic problem of the Dead Sea results from the fact that it has several inlets that flow into it — the Jordan river is one of them — but has no outlets to share its waters with other bodies. In other words: All receiving and no giving results in a body of water that has no life.

As followers of the Lord, we must never become like the Dead Sea — where all we do is sit, soak and sour! We must get rid of the desire to be a part of the "bless-me-club," and become a member of the "blessing club." The way to receive a blessing . . . is to be a blessing.

We must become an effervescent witness for Christ having a wellspring of living water flowing out of our hearts and into the lives of others. That well-spring of life, that Jesus has given to each of us as believers, is His precious Holy Spirit (see John 4:14 and John 7:37-39).

Let us determine that we shall always listen to the voice of the Holy Spirit inside us . . .

even if it means encouraging and witnessing to a pianist in the middle of a restaurant!

Chapter 7

Somebody's Children

Last summer, after sensing the need for a change of pace, my husband and I drove to Montreal, Canada, the largest French-speaking city in the world, after Paris. It was delightful and so relaxing. Just what we needed. The people were friendly, the old city intriguing, the food wonderful. Montreal is considered to be one of North America's most interesting cities. And we found it to be true. In fact, we agreed Montreal is one of the most beautiful cities we've ever seen. In two weeks' time we walked 150 miles savoring all the sights and delights, and learning about the history and the greater metropolitan area itself.

One afternoon we found an old-fashioned ice cream parlor. "It has to be a great place," Jack said, "look at all the people!" He patted his "midsection" and I raised my eyebrows and we walked in. We found an empty table and placed our order.

Just as we were being served, two bedraggled-looking young people came in each carrying a backpack. They were obviously exhausted. They spied an empty table where the waitress hadn't removed the plates from the previous customers, and they plopped down. But just that quickly, they snatched up the leftovers and wolfed them down. Eyes darting around, never making eye contact with anyone, they focused on other empty tables with plates containing food and quickly ran from one to the other, stuffing the food into their mouths. The young woman, whom I guessed to be about twenty, was more aggressive than the young man. They were just starved!

It happened so fast that everyone was in a state of shock. About the time we and others had recovered from seeing this, they grabbed their backpacks and were out of the door and gone. "Jack, if only they'd stayed long enough, we could have offered to buy them food!" I was dazed by the brief encounter. "Oh Jack," I continued, "I wonder whose child she is . . ." my voice trailed off.

Jack leaned across the table and patted my hand. The food which had been served so attractively had somehow lost its appeal. I looked around and noticed others were feeling the same way. The charming place which just moments before had been the scene of animated conversation now seemed strangely silent.

Jack's eyes were sad; mine were tearful.

As we left the ice cream parlor and continued our leisurely walk, my eyes glanced around. I was hoping to catch a glimpse of the young couple. "There are so many like them in city after city all over Canada and the United States," my husband said.

"Where are the parents?" I asked. Jack shook his head. Later, as I reflected on the incident, (in fact, I don't think I will ever forget those two young people), I was reminded that one of the most wonderful things about being a Christian is that we are God's children. Our needs are important to Him and He is always ready to supply (Phil. 4:19). He knows the way that we take (Job 23:9). I took comfort in the knowledge that God even knew their names (Isa. 45:4). I could leave them in the Father's hands.

As we venture into a new year, we can do so with confidence, knowing that the steps, as well as the stops, of God's children are ordered by Him (Ps. 37:23). Because we are His children, we can count on His promises, and they are so many! Our potential as His children is limitless.

But we need to be living up to our potential. How do people know we belong to God? Three things, it seems to me, characterize the life of a child of God: (1) Our conversation; (2) Our conduct; and (3) Our convictions.

Our conversation: *She* (or he) *openeth her mouth with wisdom; and in her tongue is the law of kindness* (Prov. 31:26).

My mother had a little saying which I have called to mind many times: "He that thinketh by the inch, and speaketh by the yard, shall be kicked by the foot."

The Bible is full of counsel about the need to guard our conversation. Consider just these few: *A soft answer turneth away wrath: but grievous words stir up anger* (Prov. 15:1). How many relationships would fare better if these words were called to mind when people were tempted to temperamental outbursts! *The tongue of the just is as choice silver: the heart of the wicked is little worth* (Prov. 10:20). Silver reflects. What a beautiful word picture this presents! Our tongues should reflect the Lord.

Our conduct: We must back up our conversation with right conduct. Those beautiful graces depicted in Galatians 5 should exemplify the conduct of our lives: *But the fruit of the Spirit is love, joy, peace, longsuffering, gentleness, goodness, faith, meekness, temperance: against such there is no law* (vv. 22, 23). An entire article could be written around each word, but let me simplify it in this way: LOVE is a new constraint, JOY is a new cheer, PEACE is a new compassion, LONG-SUFFERING is a new continuance, GENTLENESS is a new characteristic, GOODNESS is a new character, PATIENCE is a new confidence, MEEKNESS is a new courtesy and TEMPERANCE is a new contentment.

Our Convictions: The story is told of David Hume, the agnostic, who was reproached by his friends because of his inconsistency. He used to like to go hear the famous preacher John Brown preach, and when questioned about this he explained, "I don't believe all that he says, but at least once a week I like to hear a man who declares his convictions."

How important for us to have strong convictions and to abide by them. The letter of James emphasizes that our "yes" should be a simple "yes," and our "no" a simple "no" (Ja. 5:12). In other words, be convinced in your heart and stand by your convictions. Be a man or woman whose word is unquestionable. If you say you are going to do something, or you promise something, it ought to be as if you were in a courtroom and had taken an oath to speak the truth.

These are just some of the identifying

characteristics that mark us as children of God. The psalmist said, *Mark the perfect man, and behold the upright: for the end of that man is peace* (Ps. 37:37). None of us have arrived, we aren't wholly perfect, progress is perhaps a more accurate word to describe our condition. But we should be progressing.

Perhaps a good prayer would be: "Lord, help me to reflect the fact that I am your child."

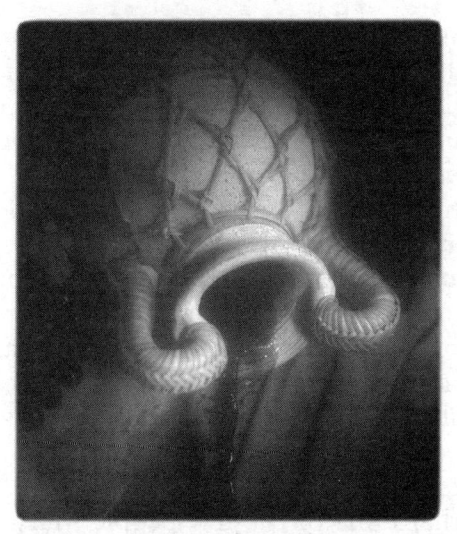

Chapter 8

Who Is Mary?

It seems to me that most Christians today — especially Protestants — spend little time thinking about Mary.

Oh, once a year she shows up on a Christmas card, shown either riding on a donkey's back or keeping a silent vigil beside the newborn Christ child in the manger. Even then, she may be scarcely noticed amid the animals, shepherds, and wise men.

On those occasions when we do think about Mary, our main concern may be maintaining the proper balance between reserve and respect for this remarkable woman. Yet we can't fully understand the miracle of the Christmas story if we fail to consider Mary's role. She's really the central human figure in one of the most important events in the history of mankind.

Who was Mary? What relevance does her life have to our personal faith?

I am astounded by her comprehension and calm acceptance of the monumental miracle the angel Gabriel announced would happen. Imagine a poor, uneducated peasant girl being told she would conceive and give birth to a great king, the Son of God! Yet Mary understood . . . and she believed.

Perhaps one of the few people Mary could confide in during this time was her cousin, Elisabeth, who was to be the mother of John the Baptist. Elisabeth confirmed that what was happening to Mary was divinely ordained, and encouraged her. *Blessed is she that believed,* said Elisabeth, *for there shall be a performance of those things which were told her from the Lord* (Luke 1:45).

In the midst of today's relaxed (collapsed?) moral standards, it may be difficult for us to realize the sacrifice Mary had to make to agree to yield herself to the Holy Spirit. In her culture, for an unmarried woman to be found with child could have resulted in a death sentence!

At the very least, she faced misunderstanding by most people, probably rejection by her betrothed, and scorn and shame in the eyes of her contemporaries.

Which of us would have the courage and strength to subject ourselves to such an ordeal? But Mary's strong faith moved her to cooperate with God's plan. Her simple, humble response was, *Be it unto me according to thy word* (Luke 1:38).

Mary stands out in the gospel story as the symbol of the true humanity of Jesus. She is the link between the divinity of Christ and the humanity of Jesus. She is the link between the divinity of Christ and the humanity of all mankind. Jesus could not have been completely God and completely man without Mary's role.

Without question Mary and her husband, Joseph, played an important role in shaping and influencing the developing years of the young Jesus. As a youngster, Jesus was taught the scriptures and the laws of God. When He amazed the learned scholars in Jerusalem at age 12, one can say that His divinity shone through . . . but He also had been taught and trained to do His homework.

And it may well have been at home that Jesus learned the words He cried at Gethsemane — "Not my will, but thine be done!" Certainly His mother had set an example before Him of humble submission to the plan of God.

The character exemplified in the life of

Mary is an inspiration and challenge to every believer. She was courageous, committed, compassionate, and concerned.

Mary's Courage

I envision Mary having great strength and durability, yet retaining complete and perfect femininity. She was courageous, going calmly and with dignity where few others would have been willing to go. She faced hardship, opposition, even danger, with no complaints. She was willing to let God's will be done in her life.

After facing the ostracism and personal humiliation of being pregnant without a husband, Mary had the strength and courage to mount a donkey only a few days before giving birth and make the long, hard journey to Bethlehem.

And it must have taken courage of another kind to deal with the throngs of strangers who came to visit her newborn son — shepherds, wise men from the East, and doubtless other curious onlookers.

Later, when Herod sought to kill all babies in the land, she helped save Jesus from the slaughter by journeying to Egypt with Joseph and the child to live among foreigners. Did this take courage? Absolutely!

And let's not forget the courage demanded of Mary to take on the responsibility for rearing and nurturing Jesus through his childhood and into manhood. It takes great courage to be the parent of any child — how much more to be the mother of the Son of God?

Mary's Commitment

Once Mary heard and responded to the angel's announcement that she was chosen for a divine commission, she was committed. From that moment on, she never wavered or looked back.

Her commitment was complete — she set aside any personal ambitions and dreams to make herself available to God's plan. Her whole life was dedicated to carrying out the divine mission to which God had called her.

So seriously did she take her responsibility that the crisis of losing and finding her Son again in Jerusalem when He was 12 prompted her to scold Him for causing her such concern. And Jesus gently rebuked her by reminding her that He must be about His Father's business.

And a few years later, at Calvary, her commitment kept her at the front of the cross while almost everyone else fled. Even in the face of what must have been tremendous anguish to see her Son's suffering, she remained committed to God's plan.

Mary's Compassion

From the beginning of her adult life, Mary

lived her life for others. She put the needs of others before her own, and ministered to those around her — husband, family, friends.

I imagine Mary as being the perfect embodiment of all the marvelous qualities of the virtuous wife described in Proverbs 31. She was humble, but supremely capable and efficient in her efforts to serve.

Can you imagine this woman going around very arrogantly, saying, "Treat me special — I am the mother of the Son of God?" Of course not.

Surely Jesus patterned part of His life after her example. When he promised rest to those who labor and are heavy laden, He said, *I am meek and lowly in heart* (Matthew 11:29). I am sure He must have observed the qualities of humility and compassion in her daily life.

Mary's Concern for Others

The story of Christ's first miracle in turning water into wine at the wedding in Cana provides a very telling insight into the character of the mother of Jesus. Even in a situation where providing the refreshments was not her responsibility, Mary was concerned for others. When it became obvious that there was not enough to drink at the wedding feast and the host was about to be embarrassed, she got involved.

She was aware of what was going on around her . . . and was concerned about the problems of others. But more than feeling sympathy for them, she had a solution. "I know my Son can take care of this," she said.

After making Jesus aware of the problem, she told the servants of the house, *Whatsoever He saith unto you, do it* (John 2:5). And, of course, the Lord did meet the need and the beverage He provided was recognized as the best of the evening!

So Mary's life is an inspiration to us — her courage, commitment, compassion, and concern. Her Christian character and devotion is an eloquent witness that, with the help of the Holy Spirit, we can be strong enough to withstand any test, even the crucifying tensions of modern life. Perhaps the key to Mary's spiritual life is found in that beautiful Bible passage known as the Magnificat (see Luke 1:46-53). In those wonderful verses it seems one can hear her opening her innermost heart as she cries — "My soul doth magnify the Lord, and my spirit hath rejoiced in God my Savior . . . holy is His name. And His mercy is on them that fear Him from generation to generation."

Thank you, Mary, for the inspiration and godly example of your faith-filled life! May God help us to magnify the Lord, rejoice in our spirits, and receive His mercy . . . today, and until His perfect plan is fulfilled in all the earth.

Chapter 9

Eat, Drink and Be Merry

"Happy New Year!" "Eat, drink, and be merry . . . have a good time!"

Each year, when the waning hours of December give way to the opening moments of January, millions of people around the world celebrate. Many attend parties, some lavish extravaganzas with feasts and open bars, others small private gatherings with more modest refreshments.

Restaurants and nightclubs are filled to capacity, and multitudes gather in New York City's Time Square to wait for and watch the fall of a large, lighted globe which symbolizes the passing of the old year into history and the arrival of the future in the form of the New Year.

At the stroke of midnight, millions lift their glasses for a toast to the New Year, and by word and example encourage each other to "eat, drink, and be merry!"

There are other celebrations, too, where the liquor does not flow and the merriment is not a boisterous attempt to overcome propriety and inhibitions. One could not fail to notice that the eating, drinking, and being merry in these celebrations is of quite another kind.

In thousands of churches across the country, Christians gather for "watch night" services to give thanks for God's blessings during the old year and to invoke His guidance and provision in the year to come. There is time given for fellowship, testimonies, praise and worship, prayers — for food, music, tears, joy, and laughter! Here, too, people are observing the universal invitation to eat, drink, and be merry (spiritually, as we'll see).

It should come as no surprise that Christians should be able to celebrate with genuine exuberance and joy — even more than the people of the world. Our Lord said, *These things have I spoken unto you, that my joy might remain in you, and that your joy might be full* (John 15:11).

Becoming a Christian does not take away all problems and difficulties in our lives. All of us have discovered that there are numerous occasions for unhappiness. But neither should being pious appear to be an ordeal of misery.

A keen observer once noted that sometimes Christians act like a man with a headache — he doesn't want to get rid of his head but it hurts to keep it on. Groaning, complaining, and displaying a mournful face is not the best way to express one's faith. How can Christians expect unbelievers to seek very earnestly something that looks so uncomfortable?

Jesus said, *In the world ye shall have tribulation; but be of good cheer; I have overcome the world* (John 16:33).

If we have the assurance of being overcomers with Christ, we have a right to celebrate! As Christians, we of all people should be able to say "eat, drink, and be merry."

Eat

First of all, we can eat. Our appetite should not be for caviar and other gourmet delicacies, but for the Word of God. The Apostle Peter admonishes, *As newborn babes, desire the sincere milk of the word, that ye may grow thereby* (1 Peter 2:2).

God's Word is our source for the substance of faith . . . and faith provides the strength that enables us to stand against the sea of trouble that may surround us at times.

I love the imagery of Micah 5:4, *And he*

shall stand and feed in the strength of the Lord. What a great thought — that through the Word we can feast and draw strength from the Lord.

In the original language, the meaning of the word translated "feed" also implies "to shepherdize." To me that suggests that the benefit we obtain is not just food, but also a shepherd to guide us, watch over us, restore us, protect us, and preserve us. No wonder the Lord invites us to "come and dine."

In the "Decade of Destiny," let us take advantage of the bountiful benefits God has provided for us in the Bible. Even as we daily consume physical food, every single day may we find a renewal of faith from taking in the substance of God's Word which will give us joy and provide strength for life's challenges.

Ho, every one that thirsteth, come ye to the waters (Isaiah 55:1).

Have you ever been thirsty? Surely thirst is one of the greatest discomforts the human body can endure.

I'll never forget being in Israel a few years ago to tape a television special. I was performing a song on location — out in the merciless, glaring heat of the sun on a 115+ degree day.

After a while my mouth and throat were dry and parched. My tongue actually stuck to my teeth. I was absolutely parched. Somehow I managed to get through the song, but I felt exhausted and faint, and we headed back to our hotel.

As soon as we arrived, they gave me a large glass of iced tea, and I quickly drank it down. That was several years ago, and I still remember how good that cold drink tasted. I felt like it had saved my life!

Perhaps you've had your own desert experience, when everything around you seemed dry and lifeless and you were nearly overcome with thirst. What a joy in such a time to drink of the water of the Word — to taste and see that the Lord is good!

Jesus ministered to a Samaritan woman at a well one day. After asking her for a drink from the well, He offered her a source of living water. *Whosoever drinketh of the water that I shall give him shall never thirst; but the water that I shall give him shall be in him a well of water springing up into everlasting life* (John 4:14; John 7:37).

Think of it — Christ himself, and the Holy Spirit, will well up inside of us as a source of living water that will forever quench the thirst of our souls. The water they give is permanent and satisfying!

How do we drink of this living water? By practicing His presence and spending time with Him. If we eat by reading the Word of God, then we drink by spending time in meditation and communion with the Lord in His presence.

Isaiah 12:3 says, *Therefore with joy shall ye draw water out of the wells of salvation.* All Christians have this living water inside when they receive the Lord. I do! You do! But so often we don't have the spiritual maturity that keeps that fountain of water springing forth.

People who sometimes complain that their spiritual lives have become very dry need to take that scripture to heart and draw new water from the well and renew their joy. Perhaps they have not been drawing from Him, drinking instead from some man-made well. Let's be careful what we drink, lest the water within become unfit and contaminated. It is only when we draw from Him and His Word that we allow the Holy Spirit to truly refresh us.

I believe the effect we get from drinking Christ's living water should be the same that people of the world get from drinking wine — it should bring a relaxed joy. *And be not drunk with wine, wherein is excess; but be filled with the Spirit* (Ephesians 5:18). Drinkers seem to experience an almost immediate sense of joy and happiness, just because they've been drinking. In the same way, when we drink of the water of life, people should notice that we are experiencing happiness and joy . . . because we've been drinking.

Be Merry

Jesus said in John 10:10, *I am come that they*

might have life, and that they might have it more abundantly.

Nowhere does the Bible teach that we shouldn't enjoy life. Rather, we are told that Jesus intended for us to live an abundant life. Abundance is a positive condition, suggesting satisfaction and joy.

Many in the world seem preoccupied with their pursuit of happiness. They equate happiness with hilarity — with being carefree and giddy and full of laughter.

To me, there's a difference between happiness and joy. The world's happiness is totally dependent on circumstances, on what's happening around them. But the true Christian can have joy no matter what comes his way because of the abundant life that is being poured out through him.

The Psalmist David declared, *Thou has put gladness in my heart* (Psalm 4:7). These are not the empty words of a pious Pollyanna! David knew many heartaches and disappointments in his life. He suffered the loss of a child, his own son turned against him, his king tried to kill him, his own reign was turbulent and filled with war and struggle. Certainly he didn't live a sheltered, picture-perfect life, yet he could say he had gladness. *Happy is he . . . whose hope is in the Lord his God,* he wrote in Psalm 146:5. And in the midst of life's trials, troubles, and heartaches, that is the only source for happiness.

The world's quest for happiness through eating, drinking, and being merry is doomed to failure. Following through with their formula will only cause them to wake up the next morning feeling really bad. As my husband, Jack, has often said, "If you have champagne on Saturday night, you'll have a real pain on Sunday morning."

In reality, the only people who can find true joy and happiness by following the advice to "eat, drink, and be merry" are the people of God! They partake of spiritual manna that produces true joy. Beloved friend, in these last days, don't be overcome by the darkness of the world and the doom and gloom some would promote. Eat of the promises of God's Word. Drink of the Holy Spirit's never-failing presence. Be merry with the joy of the Lord welling up within! Life is a rich adventure when we live up to our privileges and experience His unspeakable blessings.

This, then, should be our invitation to the lost and unsaved. Rather than issuing a warning to sinners to seek salvation as an escape, we can joyfully proclaim, "Come with us and we will do thee good — the Lord invites you to eat, drink, and be merry . . . for tomorrow we live!"

Chapter 10

Just to Say, "Thank You!"

No story in the Bible more movingly pictures human gratitude than the healing of ten lepers in Luke 17:12-18 . . .

And as He entered into a certain village, there met Him ten men that were lepers, which stood afar off: and they lifted up their voices and said, "Jesus, Master, have mercy on us."

And when He saw them, He said unto them, "Go shew yourselves unto the priests." And it came to pass, that, as they went, they were cleansed.

And one of them, when he saw that he was

healed, turned back, and with a loud voice glorified God. And he fell down on his face at His feet, giving Him thanks: and he was a Samaritan.

And Jesus answering said, "Were there not ten cleansed? But where are the nine? There are not found that returned to give glory to God, save this stranger."

Have you too found that sometimes when a person gets what he wants, he forgets to say thank you? Throughout Jesus' ministry, He was giving examples of how we should live. He knew — as He knew all things — that only one man would return to express appreciation. Thus, Christ wanted this story of the ten lepers recorded for future generations, so that we would know the importance of giving thanks.

Give Without Expecting Thanks?

I've heard it said that we should not "expect" thanks in return for the kindnesses we show. If we don't expect it, we will never be disappointed in our fellow man. However, I believe that the attitude of being grateful and showing it is a biblical principle. Notice verse 17; it seems as if Jesus expected a "thank-you" from all ten lepers. He said, "But where are the nine?"

Jesus was showing us a practical example of Colossians 3:15, "Be ye thankful." Obviously, thanksgiving is expected of us. This is one reason mothers and fathers, while teaching their children to speak, emphasize the importance of saying "please" and "thank you."

We expect such "common" courtesies even from toddlers. Naturally, it is disconcerting when adults are ungrateful in response to God's kindnesses to them. How many of us follow the dictum of Colossians 3:15, "Be ye thankful"?

Bless the LORD, O My Soul!

In Psalm 103, we read a beautiful song of thanksgiving:

Bless the Lord, O my soul: and all that is within me, bless His holy name.

Bless the Lord, O my soul, and forget not all His benefits:

Who forgiveth all thine iniquities; Who healeth all thy diseases;

Who redeemeth thy life from destruction; Who crowneth thee with lovingkindness and tender mercies;

Who satisfieth thy mouth with good things; so that thy youth is renewed like the eagle's. The Lord executeth righteousness . . .

(Psalm 103:1-6)

Notice in this text that the psalmist recalls the "benefits" of serving God, and even lists them in his song of praise. Have you ever created such a list? The little Sunday School song that I learned as a child implores us to "count your blessings; name them one by one, and it will surprise you what the Lord has done." When we pray and give thanks to God, let us remember all the wonderful blessings He has bestowed on us!

A Chocolate Remembrance

It was my special joy to meet and fellowship with the many friends who came to our open house at our JVI Headquarters. What a pleasure it was to hear so many of them say, "Thank you" to Dr. Van Impe and me during that great day of celebration.

Some of our friends even surprised us with special presents. I'll never forget, one beautiful little girl, maybe seven years of age, with her big eyes glowing, handed me a box of candy and said, "We remembered that your husband likes chocolates." I reached down, embraced her, and said, "Thank you, sweetheart."

Since we are unable to write thank-you notes to everyone who came to our open house or brought gifts, I would like to, in this open forum, thank everyone for their thoughtfulness, love and generosity.

But let me go one step beyond thanking our wonderful guests who came to visit us. Let me also extend my gratitude to every supporter and friend of our ministry. Thank you all, dear ones, for your financial help, prayers, letters and encouragement.

We especially thank you whose lives have

been changed for your notes and letters of testimony. Jack and I have had many praise sessions because of God's word in your hearts.

The Impact of Encouragement

It would be virtually impossible to carry on this ministry to which God has called us without help and encouragement from precious friends like you. We need your encouragement: we thrive upon hearing about your triumphs and victories because God used our ministry to reach you. It is difficult to express the impact we feel as we receive hundreds of thousands of letters each year sharing such blessings. It is like a warm ray of sunshine on a cold winter's day.

At His last supper, Jesus showed us exactly how important encouragement is at the darkest hours of our life. When Jesus had thus said, He was troubled in spirit, and testified, and said, "Verily, verily, I say unto you, that one of you shall betray me." Then the disciples looked one on another, doubting of whom He spake. Now there was leaning on Jesus' bosom one of His disciples, whom Jesus loved (John 13:21-23).

John could feel the Master's burdened spirit and leaned his head on Jesus to express his love and concern. John wanted to give his Lord a measure of additional strength and encouragement. This example of human love from this disciple is so beautiful that it cannot be overlooked.

I am sure Jesus absorbed a great deal of love and respect from His apostles. I do believe, however, God laid it on their hearts to be extremely compassionate and supportive of the Lord Jesus especially because of the agony which lay ahead.

The Most Important Person on Earth

Jack and I thank you for the encouragement you have been to us. May our example help you to express appreciation to special people in your life for the blessings they have been to you.

For instance, when was the last time you said "thank you" to the person you hold dearest on earth? Remember your mate is a gift from God, and the Bible teaches us to love and respect each other. Read Ephesians 5:20, 25, 28.

Ladies, when the man in your life opens the door for you, do you say, "Thank you, sweetheart"? Gentlemen, when the lady of your dreams fixes your favorite meal, do you remember to say, "Thank you honey, that was delicious!" (You might even say "thank you" when the roast is tough, especially when you have only been married for 10 weeks!) When your son or daughter plans a surprise birthday party for you, do you give him or her a loving hug and express gratitude? Oh how important it is to be mindful to say "thank you," especially to those closest to us.

Thanks for the Memories

Parents, also, deserve our thanks. In fact, the edict to honor our father and mother is one of the Ten Commandments — and it is the first commandment with a promise. *Honor thy father and thy mother: that thy days may be long upon the land which the Lord thy God giveth thee* (Exodus 20:12).

I am sure that there are many people who made an infinitely important impact upon your life, but who probably are not aware of it. Perhaps there was a teacher somewhere along the line who captured your imagination and helped you to learn. Would it not be a wonderful idea to write a thank-you note telling him or her of the great contribution that they made toward the success of your career and personal life?

I heard the story of a grown man who remembered his best school teacher from years past, and sent her a letter thanking her for all she had given him and his classmates. The teacher was in her 80's now, and gratefully replied, saying: "I taught school for 50 years, and this is the first note of gratitude I have ever received!"

Likewise, your thank-you note would mean so much to someone today.

Everyday Gratitude

Most of us don't take the time to thank our pastors or Sunday School teachers or ministers of music and youth for the hours they spent studying and preparing to help us in our spiritual walk. I feel confident they would appreciate knowing you are grateful and have been blessed by their ministry.

Saying "thank-you" will also enhance your opportunities to witness for Christ. When the clerk at the supermarket is helpful, look that person right in the eye and say, "Thank you."

I know this is appreciated, because one young lady who has helped me many times at the store said to me, "You know, Rexella, you are the only customer who really looks at me, and this tells me I'm important to you." I pray she sees more than just a look, but that through my eyes she sees Someone who cares for her deeply.

Of course, we could go on and on with a list of people who deserve our thanks, but as you open your horizon of opportunities to show appreciation, let me assure you that you will experience a great sense of satisfaction in expressing it.

H.W. Beecher said, "Pride slays thanksgiving. A proud man never thinks he gets as much as he deserves."

The Bible tells us that all have sinned and fallen short of the glory of God. In light of eternity, none of us "deserves" the many wonderful blessings which have been bestowed on us. Our sinful humanity deserves only eternal punishment.

Yet Christ in His infinite mercy provided a way of escape for us through His shed blood, and rewards us with eternal life. How can we not be thankful every moment of our lives? We did nothing to deserve all of His blessing; Christ did it all.

So there is no room for pride in our lives, and oh — so much room for thanksgiving! Let us rejoice this day and obey the command of Colossians 3:15: "Be ye thankful."

Chapter 11

Go Home a Winner

During the course of a year, Jack and I receive various invitations to speak at a variety of functions. One such invitation that he never refuses is the privilege of being the keynote speaker for an international prophecy conference in Florida. The invitation came again this year; he accepted, and we were on our way! Flying to Tampa would surely be the quickest means of getting there, but since we desperately needed a break from our workload, we decided to incorporate a few days of relaxation by driving to our destination. I was elated to see the bright and beautiful February morning as we left our home in Michigan. We thoroughly enjoyed the quiet, pleasant, and fun-filled days on the road. It was a perfect time to talk with each other without interruptions and absorb some of God's magnificent, majestic creation.

As we approached Atlanta, Georgia, I was especially taken with a sign on the back of a Yellow Checker taxi. It was an interesting slogan that said, "Go home a winner; play the Lottery!" The first four words began to echo in my mind and heart, "Go home a winner!" I prayed silently, "Lord, this is what you expect from all of your followers. You want us to be winners in the race of life."

Remembering that heaven is a prepared place for a prepared people, we must truly be ready to go home by knowing the Lord Jesus as Savior (Philippians 3:10). When this is a reality, we will have the blessing of God's Spirit within our hearts (Romans 8:9). Surely it is impossible to be successful in attaining the approval of our Lord unless we have the power of His Spirit in our lives. He alone enables us to win the battle against Satan.

I do not need to convince any thinking person that we are fighting against some fierce odds. All we need to do is watch the television news or read daily newspapers and current magazines to see how Satan is winning in some arenas of the world. Thank the Lord that it is possible for us to say, as did the Apostle Paul:

I have fought a good fight, I have finished my course, I have kept the faith (I Timothy 4:7).

Here are some of the thoughts that I had pertaining to being a winner as we continued our journey South.

1. Follow the Lord in His example of holiness.

There are several ways that we can go home a winner. One would certainly be by following the Lord Jesus in His example of holy living.

Positionally, we have been declared holy because of what Jesus did for us when He died at Calvary, but experientially, God wants us to follow peace and holiness in our daily lives. How good that our loving God gave us the Ten Commandments (not suggestions) so that we could have guidelines to help us know right and wrong, black and white, and not the modern concept of living in some gray area of life with no absolutes. Often we hear a theory called "situation ethics" expounded. This contemporary humanistic reasoning manifests itself when one accepts this theory which declares: "I have the right to ignore God's commandments because of the situation in which I find myself." This philosophy offers no restraints for moral actions or personal pleasures.

There are times, however, when we are unable to live completely like the Lord would desire, and we fall short of His holy example.

How good to know that we do serve a loving, forgiving God. The Apostle John tells us the story of a woman who was caught in the act of adultery and thrown at Jesus' feet. She was guilty of a great, and immoral sin — according to Jewish law she deserved death, but Jesus' response to her was one of overwhelming love. The power of His love is greater than any sin. He not only forgave her, but he would not allow her accusers to condemn her. He knew they too were guilty and hypocritical about their condemnation. Thus he looked at her with compassion and said, *Neither do I condemn thee: go, and sin no more* (John 8:11). Quickly notice however, that even though Jesus loved and forgave her of her immorality, He also exhorted her not to allow the sin to continue.

In the same way, you and I stand forgiven . . . but He expects us to live a holy lifestyle.

2. Follow the Lord in His example of humility.

This is a staggering and astounding admonition when we consider a very important aspect about our Lord as He walked among us.

He was not an ordinary man or prophet. He was the Son of God! A member of the Holy Trinity! Scripture reveals to us that He helped to create the heavens and the earth — and that nothing was made without Him

(Colossians 1:16). He, as God, is omnipotent, omnipresent, and omniscient. With this in mind, I am in awe to think that when He walked upon earth He gave us an amazing example of humility.

I find it hard to comprehend that He was so humble He knelt down and washed the feet of His disciples (John 13:14). What a beautiful and awesome thought: We serve a humble God!

Surely this example should cause us to conclude that the more responsibility you and I are given in this life . . . the more humility is required. Perhaps the reason some hesitate to exemplify humility is found in the fact that they confuse meekness with weakness. Meekness never manifests itself in weakness.

I am so grateful that I have had the privilege of working alongside so many great men. In my opinion, the greatest of these personalities were those who chose to humble themselves in the sight of God, following the Lord Jesus in His meek and lowly life (Matthew 11:28 and 29). In so doing, God exalted and blessed these leaders abundantly (James 4:10).

An astounding illustration of this can be found in Westminster Abbey in London, England. There, among the tombs of many, are the tributes to David Livingstone and his brother.

David Livingstone's brother was a man of great fame since he was a very successful business man. When David Livingstone wanted to go to the mission field to share the Gospel, it was his brother who tried to reason with him by saying, "Don't go David, you are burying yourself in Africa and wasting your life. You have so much to look forward to in England. In a short time you are destined to become wealthy." David Livingstone listened to the voice of God instead of his brother. He left for the mission field to pioneer a tremendous work for His Lord in Central Africa.

Today, on the monument of David Livingstone, there is a beautiful, royal tribute etched in stone as a commemoration of his tremendous and enduring accomplishments. Right next to this tribute, lies the monument of his brother that merely reads: "The brother of David Livingstone."

We may never receive the promised exaltation of James 4:10 here on earth, but someday we will go home winners if we exemplify humility in our lives.

3. Follow the Lord in His example of Evangelization.

A dramatic and dynamic event occurred when Jesus ascended into heaven. The last words that He spoke to his disciples were: *But ye shall receive power, after that the Holy Ghost is come upon you: and ye shall be witnesses unto me both in Jerusalem, and in all Judea, and in*

Samaria, and unto the uttermost part of the earth (Acts 1:8). Let's consider two thoughts concerning His last request.

Why do we receive power? So we can witness. Where did Jesus want us to witness? Right where we are. Perhaps another way we could paraphrase this is: "But ye shall receive power, after that the Holy Ghost is come upon you: and ye shall be witnesses unto me both in Detroit, and in all of Michigan, and in the United States, and unto the uttermost part of the earth." Place your city, state and nation in the above.

I appreciate how Jesus prepared lives around Him for His message of love and salvation. First of all, He cared for the specific needs of each and every one. Remember how he healed their bodies (John 5:1-9), how He brought comfort to their minds during times of sorrow (John 11:20-45), and how He gave them food to satisfy their hunger (Matthew 15:32-38). It may prove a blessing for us to follow His example by caring for those around us before we attempt to reach out to them spiritually. There are so many with multiplied problems. Let's always be aware of their needs first and then love them enough to reach out in a tangible way.

Secondly, He met the needs of those near Him as well as far away. He blessed and redeemed His disciples and ultimately the souls of the world via Calvary. Our mission field is all around us. Let's be vigilant and ready to help those at home as well as those abroad. Sometimes those closest to us are neglected. Perhaps we could say we are often too far-sighted.

Once there was a young lady in San Francisco who wanted to go to China as a missionary. But when she went before the Missions Board, they asked her two very important questions . . . The first was: "How far do you live from Chinatown?" "Just a few miles . . . " she replied. Then they asked her the second question: "Have you been there to share the Gospel with them?" Her answer was "no." How sad! The board in good conscience could not approve her application to become a missionary.

Take note! The last thing Jesus asked us to do before He ascended into heaven was, "Go and be witnesses." The first thing we will be asked by the Lord when we arrive home is: "Did you keep my commandment?" Scripture tells us there will be a special reward for such an effort (I Thessalonians 2:19).

John the Baptist spoke these inspiring words that may help us in our efforts to be winners. He said of Jesus, *He must increase, but I must decrease* (John 3:30). May this powerful exhortation reside and reign in our hearts as we resolve to "GO HOME A WINNER!"

Chapter 12

You Are God's Gift to a Lost World

Did you ever realize that you are God's gift to your world? He has planted you on this earth like a precious flower to share the beautiful scent of salvation with people in the parched desert around you. He gave you as a gift to these souls in need, and He expects you not only to brighten their world, but to bear fruit of new souls won to His kingdom. It's not difficult to do when you allow the Holy Spirit to work through you.

People all around you need hope. You can tell, just reading the newspaper. I read several periodicals every week, just to keep current on world events . . . And I can't help but notice that so many articles in the papers point to despair.

Violent crime is on the rise. Unemployment and poverty are rampant. Even suicide — which used to be so rare — is becoming commonplace. It breaks my heart to read that suicide is one of the leading causes of death among teenagers. Now even children are following this deadly trend, like the little girl we read about in Florida. She threw herself in front of a train because her mother was dying with the AIDS virus.

Yet every time I read a newspaper item like this, it just rings an alarm bell in my heart that says: People need HOPE. They need the truth of God's love. "We have this hope as an anchor for the soul, firm and secure." We read about the love of God in Hebrews 6:19. That hope is our anchor, and God is calling each one of us to share that hope with souls in danger around us. Jesus has chosen you and me as His gift to a lost and dying world, to share his eternal love.

I know that you prize soul-winning above every other calling in your life; you have demonstrated that by your strong support of this ministry, which is sharing God's love continually with those in need. Yet I also believe that God has called each one of His children to share His precious salvation message in our personal lives. How can we do it? How can we find the words?

The Lord knows you inside and out; He knows you better than you know yourself. Through His intimate knowledge of your special talents and your limitations, I believe He will call you to win souls in the best, most effective way possible for you ... What I mean is, God does not expect you to become an evangelist or a Gospel singer or a street-corner preacher. He simply calls you to do what you are able to do in presenting a Gospel witness.

For instance, there's a little shopping mall near my home where I like to browse when I can spare a few minutes. I don't go there with my Bible under my arm, looking for someone I could talk to ... I simply go shopping like any other lady. But the Lord has given me opportunities to witness to several of the workers at that mall — waitresses and sales ladies.

Sometimes one of them will say, "Why are you always so happy? There's something different about you." They don't care whether or not I've been to Bible school or what church I attend. They just notice God's love at work in me. Or sometimes if I ask one of them how they're doing, they will say, "I'm having a problem . . ." and they pour out their hearts to me.

They sense my love and interest in their lives, and they want to know what makes me happy. Through these simple things, the Lord has allowed me to lead several of these ladies to the cross and pray with them to accept Jesus. It's not difficult, and it doesn't require that you know a lot of Scripture or have a powerful testimony.

I would encourage you to use our video teachings in your personal witnessing. Invite your neighbors to a Bible study in your home, and use Jack's video teaching as a guide — or give our videos as a gift. It's a loving and effective way to warn your friends about the coming end times and lead them to Jesus.

I know from my own personal experience that there is something YOU can do for the Lord. You can personally witness to others and help lead them to Christ, in a specific way which God has enabled you to share and which no one else on earth could do like you. You are God's gift to a lost world — let Him use you to reach your world with His good news!

Chapter 13

A Blaze of Glory

That day is coming, dear one . . . The day we shall see Christ as He is. At that final moment of earth history for us, will He find us blazing bright with His message of love and hope?

I think of the maple trees across the street from our house. One autumn season, what a glorious display of red, yellow, brown and purple we were treated to when those leaves began to turn! When the evening sun came shining through the leaf-covered boughs, each tree seemed to be on fire.

When I was home, I enjoyed looking over

at those glorious maples. I was a little sad when the last leaves fell and only skeleton-like arms were left silhouetted against the winter sky.

I waited for spring and new leaves on those trees, but the new buds never sprouted. I was shocked to see my neighbor cutting down the lifeless limbs and dead trunks.

How could trees that had been so beautiful just last fall be dead in spring? Someone explained to me what had happened: the trees sense when they are in their last season, and they pour all their remaining strength into one last spectacular display —

They go out in a blaze of glory!

Like nature, the Bible is full of examples of this final "blaze of glory." Think of Samson, whose entire existence was reduced to turning a grind stone for the Philistines, in his eternally dark, blind state.

Yet when he was brought into the Philistine coliseum to entertain them, the Bible says:

And Samson took hold of the two middle pillars upon which the house stood, and on which it was borne up, of the one with his right hand, and of the other with his left. And Samson said, "Let me die with the Philistines." And he bowed himself with all his might; and the house fell upon the lords, and upon all the people that were therein. So the dead which he slew at his death were more than they which he slew in his life (Judges 16:29-30).

At the wedding in Cana of Galilee, Jesus turned water into wine when the bridegroom ran out of wine. And his guests declared: *Every man at the beginning doth set forth good wine; and when men have well drunk, then that which is worse: but thou hast kept the good wine until now* (John 2:10).

Job had a full, rich life until tragedy struck him. Then he went through some of the most trying times ever endured by a human being, but he stayed true to God, and it was said of him, *So the Lord blessed the latter end of Job more than his beginning* (Job 42:12).

There is a tremendous lesson for all of us in this. Without a doubt, we are living in the last season of this old world. All the prophetic signs tell us time will soon wind down. In the short time left to us, we as Christians should be like the maple tree and prepare to end this final season in a blaze of glory!

Think of it! We're in the last harvest of souls this world will ever see before Jesus comes. *Say not ye, There are yet four months, and then cometh harvest? behold, I say unto you, Lift up your eyes, and look on the fields; for they are white already to harvest* (John 4:35).

Knowing the season, we must expend every resource and every bit of strength at our disposal to light up the world with the reflected glory of our Savior. Let us shine our brightest today . . . Show our truest colors now. There will not be another season.

Wife and mother, this may be the last month or week . . . or day you will spend with your family. Pour out your love on your husband and children. Husband and father, this may be your last opportunity to make your home a glorious place to live, full of joy and love and excitement. Do it now!

Dear friend, how can you go out with a blaze of glory? There are simple acts of kindness you can do: a heart-felt compliment, a word of encouragement, a friendly phone call to a lonely acquaintance. They may be little things, but like each individual maple leaf, they can fill your life-tree full!

Dr. Van Impe and I need your continued prayer support as we try to make this season of our ministry the most glorious of all and proclaim to the world: Jesus is coming soon — perhaps today! The Scripture says . . .

For the Lord himself shall descend from heaven with a shout, with the voice of the archangel, and with the trump of God: and the dead in Christ shall rise first: Then we which are alive and remain shall be caught up together with them in the clouds, to meet the Lord in the air: and so shall we ever be with the Lord ... For yourselves know perfectly that the day of the Lord so cometh as a thief in the night (1 Thessalonians. 4:16-5:2).

Remember to pray for us, even as we pray for you. Ask God to give us so much strength, energy, vision and anointing that, like Job, the end of our lives will be greater than the beginning. As the Scriptures tell and as the signs of the times clearly show, the coming of our Lord is at hand. Let's rise to meet Him in joy and triumph, going up in a blaze of glory!

Chapter 14

Is There Room in Your Heart for Him?

Jesus came as a baby, humbling Himself to a manger, and one day, to Calvary's tree for you and me. Oh, what love!

I wonder if we can really understand the emotion in heaven and the joy on earth as Mary and Joseph made their way to Bethlehem just prior to the birth of Christ.

Can you see them as they wearily make their way through the narrow streets of the city. Mary, tired from the long journey, clings wearily to the little donkey she rides as Joseph leads it along.

Their journey is almost over, and none too

soon. They stop in front of the inn. With a tender word, Joseph comforts his wife and then strides quickly toward the inn door.

Joseph knocks at the innkeeper's door. A Baby is about to be born — the most important baby ever to be born on this earth. But the Bible tells us there was no room for them in the inn (Luke 2:7).

No room! Those are heart-rending words. Would we have said that? We wish we could push back the hands of time and make the scenario different — as they did in a school Christmas play I heard about.

One high-spirited little boy had been given the role of the innkeeper in the pageant. His parents and teachers were so excited for him, because he was a mischievous child and didn't receive many accolades.

His were simple lines. When Joseph knocked at the door and asked for a room, the innkeeper had only to say, "There is no room in the inn."

Practice performances went well. The big night came. Then came the innkeeper's moment. Knock . . . knock . . . knock — Joseph knocks at the door. With great emotion, Joseph presents his plight to the innkeeper: his wife is about to give birth; they have traveled so far; they are tired and hungry . . . Won't the innkeeper please let them in?

The little innkeeper, who had rehearsed his

lines so carefully, listened patiently. Then, loud and clear, he delivered his line: "There is no room in the inn."

Joseph turned, his shoulders sagging. But before he could leave, the innkeeper opened the door, thrust his head out, and said, "Wait! Wait! You can have my room!"

It wasn't in the script, but it was the right answer.

It wasn't in the script on that first Christmas, either. Instead, someone tapped Joseph on his sagging shoulder and said, "There's a place, if your wife won't mind. I know I can fix it and make it clean. It will at least be quiet there — and warm."

Joseph's heart must have been torn. His beloved Mary in a barn? The Son of God born in a stable? The Lord of all heaven and earth was about to make His human presence known in the world — but in a barn? This was not the birthplace Joseph had imagined for JESUS.

Yet isn't it a picture of the way Jesus is born still today, into our hearts? He is the Lord and Creator of all heaven and earth. Surely the shabby stable of our hearts is not the home He would choose for Himself? Indeed, He would have no other!

We are all innkeepers, with room for many things, but do we have room for Him? His birth in a stable was a symbol that God's love would be born anywhere — and go to any lengths — to save the precious souls of humans like you and me, if only we open our hearts to Him.

And so it was that . . . she brought forth her firstborn Son, and wrapped Him in swaddling clothes, and laid Him in a manger; because there was no room for them in the inn (Luke 2:6,7).

As we recall this most beautiful Bible story, may your heart be reminded of the importance of this season — not simply gifts, Christmas trees, families, and loved ones — but the true message of Christmas: God's never-ending love for us.